For my family: Dao, Benjamin, and Shannon

Acknowledgments

Once again I'd like to thank Sheryl Olinsky Borg and David Clark for truly believing in this project and helping to make it a reality; Lise Minovitz for her extraordinary revision of this text; Arthur Gribben for his excellent insight and comments; Dennis Oliver for his continuous help and encouragement; and the staff and students of the best ESL program in the world, California State University, Northridge!

Cheers,

Dave

Contents

READING/WRITING	CULTURE
Reading and writing e-mail messages Writing a paragraph or essay about a key pal	Exchanging e-mail with someone from a different culture
Reading about amusement parks Writing an amusement park Web site review	Learning about amusement parks around the world
Reading about existing and extinct animals Writing a paragraph or essay about animal sounds	Comparing how different languages express animal sounds
Reading about buildings and monuments Writing a paragraph or essay about a skyscraper	Learning about architecture in different countries
Reading about famous artists Writing an art review	Learning about artists around the world
Reading about Western and Chinese astrology Writing a paragraph or essay about one's horoscope	Comparing Western and Chinese astrology
Reading about different cities Writing a travel brochure and a city Web site review	Exploring cities from different countries
Reading about the United Nations Writing a paragraph or essay about a country	Learning about the United Nations
Reading about infamous criminals Writing a paragraph or essay about a crime	Exploring crime and punishment in different countries

READING/WRITING	CULTURE
Reading about proverbs, folk tales, and gestures Writing a paragraph or essay about a cultural group	Learning about customs around the world
Reading about specialized education Writing a paragraph or essay about a specific course	Learning about education in different countries
Reading family and wedding home pages Writing a paragraph or essay about a wedding custom	Exploring wedding customs from different countries
Reading about foods and restaurants Reading and writing recipes	Learning about typical meals around the world
Following on-line game directions Writing a paragraph or essay about computer games	Comparing popular games around the world
Finding information about explorers and geography Writing a paragraph or essay about geography	Exploring geography around the world
Reading about diet, ailments, and exercise Writing a paragraph or essay about exercise	Exploring different attitudes toward health, diet, and exercise
Reading about history Writing a paragraph or essay about a historical event	Exploring the history of different countries
Reading about holidays Writing a holiday Web site review	Learning about different national and religious holidays
Reading a Web-published story Summarizing a favorite novel	Learning about authors around the world
Researching prices on the Web Writing a paragraph or essay about shopping	Learning about prices and currencies in different countries

READING/WRITING	CULTURE
Reading about movies and movie stars Writing a movie review	Exploring different movie preferences
Reading about songs and types of music Writing a paragraph or essay about a musician	Exploring different types of world music
Reading a newspaper article Summarizing a newspaper article	Learning about newspapers from different countries
Reading about famous people Writing a paragraph or essay about an admired person	Learning about famous people around the world
Reading about scientists, discoveries, and inventions Writing a paragraph or essay about a scientific field	Exploring scientific discoveries around the world
Reading about sports and the Olympics Writing a paragraph or essay about a sport	Learning about sports around the world
Reading about different automobiles Writing a paragraph or essay about an automobile	Learning about transportation in different countries
Scanning for hotel and flight information Writing a paragraph or essay about a vacation	Exploring international travel
Reading about extreme weather conditions Writing a paragraph or essay about the weather	Comparing the weather in different countries
Reading job advertisements Writing a paragraph or essay about an ideal job	Identifying jobs around the world

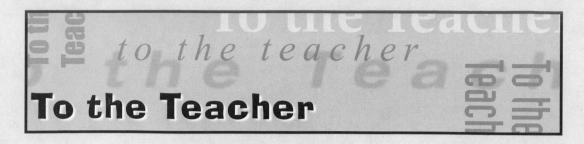
BEGIN: http://www.prenhall.com/sperling

FROM: Dave Sperling

TO: The Teacher

SUBJECT: Hello from cyberspace!

Please don't be afraid of this book! I often meet teachers who are still afraid of computers and the Internet, so I'd like to share a secret with you. The Internet is a fun, exciting, and extremely powerful learning tool for you and your students, and you'll find that it's easy to use! I made this discovery back in 1995 when I reluctantly (yes, I said reluctantly!) introduced my ESL students at California State University, Northridge, to the Internet. There, I taught them the basics of using e-mail and creating Web pages. What were the results?

- My students found the Internet fun and "cool."
- My students were thrilled to share their creativity with the entire world.
- My students increased their reading and vocabulary in English because they were exploring the World Wide Web and discovering material that interested them.
- My students were writing e-mail messages in English every day.
- My students were meeting and communicating with other students from around the world.
- My students were becoming more motivated and excited about learning English.
- My students were actually coming to class early!

The results were amazing. I was hooked, my students were hooked, and I think you and your students will be too.

This program has two components which are used together: *Dave Sperling's Internet Activity Workbook* and the companion Web site. The workbook is divided into 30 theme-based chapters, which can be used in any order. The companion Web site, at the URL above, provides links to the Web pages needed to complete the activities in the workbook. It guides the students through the Internet as they explore a variety of topics and learn English.

Since the themes in this book are featured in most ESL textbooks, *Dave Sperling's Internet Activity Workbook* makes a great supplement. I think you'll find it flexible, fun, and easy to use. Of course, I am always open to your feedback and suggestions, and would love to hear about your experiences using this workbook and the companion Web site. You can always e-mail me at sperling@eslcafe.com.

By choosing this book, you should consider yourself an ESL/EFL Internet pioneer!

All the best,

Dave Sperling

California State University, Northridge
March 1999

BEGIN: `http://www.prenhall.com/sperling`

FROM: Dave Sperling

TO: The Student

SUBJECT: Let's get started!

Fasten your seat belts and hold on tight, because we're about to begin an exciting Internet adventure. Soon, you'll be using the Internet to improve your English and communicate with new on-line friends.

Searching the Web

To make your ride a little smoother, you'll need to learn some Internet basics. The **World Wide Web** (or the **Web**) is part of the **Internet**. It consists of millions of documents called **Web pages**.

To access the Web you'll need a **Web browser**. This is a program that allows you to navigate and view the World Wide Web. Two popular Web browsers are:

- **Microsoft Internet Explorer**
  http://www.microsoft.com/ie
- **Netscape Navigator**
  http://home.netscape.com

Web browsers allow you to navigate the World Wide Web and explore **Web sites**. When you use your mouse to click on a **hyperlink** (or **link**), you can, for example, read the latest news from your country, chat with friends around the globe, view paintings from world-famous art galleries, and listen to the latest pop music.

There are a vast number of Web sites on the World Wide Web. To help you find information quickly and easily, **search engines** can help you search by **category**.

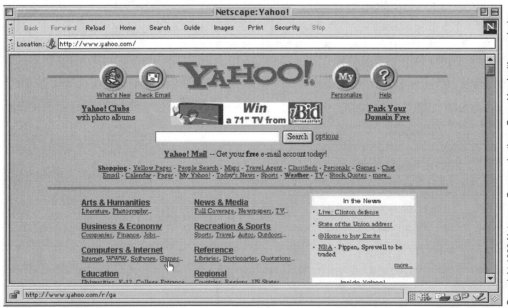

You can also search by **key word**. If your search brings up too many Web sites, you can narrow your topic and search again.

boats	Search

sailboats	Next Search

Some of my favorite search engines are:
- **Alta Vista**
  http://www.altavista.com
- **Hotbot**
  http://www.hotbot.com
- **Metacrawler**
  http://www.go2net.com/search.html
- **Yahoo**
  http://www.yahoo.com

As you learn to **surf** (or search) the Net, you will need to learn some specialized words:
- **bookmark** A marker that enables you to return to a Web page at a later date.
- **home page** The main Web page of an individual, group, or organization.
- **URL** Uniform Resource Locator, pronounced U-R-L. An address on the World Wide Web. For example, `http://www.eslcafe.com` is the URL of my home page, Dave's ESL Café.

You can find other specialized words in the **Glossary of Internet Terms** on pages 142 and 143. You can also look them up in an on-line or regular dictionary.

Sending and Receiving E-mail

The Internet allows you to exchange **e-mail**, or electronic mail. This is a great way to practice your writing in English. Once you get used to sending and receiving messages instantly, **snail mail** (or mail delivered by the post office) will seem very slow.

Tip: You can get a free Web-based e-mail account that is accessible from any computer in the world that is connected to the Internet. Popular Web sites for free e-mail include:
- **Hotmail**
  http://www.hotmail.com
- **RocketMail**
  http://www.rocketmail.com

Before you send a message, you need to know the recipient's e-mail address. An e-mail address has three parts:

$$\underset{1}{\underline{\text{username}}} \; \underset{2}{\underline{@}} \; \underset{3}{\underline{\text{domainname}}}$$

1. Your user name is your unique name on an Internet provider. My user name is `sperling`.
2. @ is the "at" symbol and is needed on every e-mail address after the user name.
3. The domain name is the address of the Internet provider. My domain name is `eslcafe.com`.

Therefore, my e-mail address is `sperling@eslcafe.com`. Note that e-mail addresses have no spaces between letters, and that spelling is important. If you make a mistake, your message will **bounce** back to you and never reach the recipient.

At the top of each email message are the following elements: **To**, **Subject**, and **Cc**.

TO:	sperling@eslcafe.com
SUBJECT:	Question About Your Book
CC:	teacher@englishschool.edu

In the **To** space, enter the recipient's e-mail address. In the **Subject** space, enter the topic of your message. If you want another person to receive a copy of your message (perhaps your teacher), enter that person's e-mail address in the **Cc** space.

You can practice by sending me an e-mail message at `sperling@eslcafe.com`. I promise to write you back!

Smileys (Emoticons)

Since most communication on the Net is done with text, you can't see the other person's body language or facial expressions. By adding **Smileys**, or **emoticons**, you can show how you feel about a topic or subject. To read the expression, tilt your head to the left. Here is a short list of some of my favorites:

:-)	smile	:-(	frown	;-)	wink
:-]	bigger smile	:-[	bigger frown	:-0	shock
:-D	laughter	>:-<	anger	|-)	sleeping

Try adding one or two Smileys to your messages.

Netiquette

Netiquette, or Net etiquette, is very important for the **newbie** (new user) to learn. Remember these DOs and DON'Ts:

DOs
- Be polite. Respect the recipient's feelings and opinions.
- Be clear. This will help prevent misunderstandings.
- Add your name (or signature) to the end of an e-mail message.
- Check your spelling.

DON'Ts
- Avoid **spamming**. Don't send the same message to many people.
- Avoid **flaming**. Don't get into on-line arguments.
- Avoid **shouting**. DON'T WRITE YOUR ENTIRE MESSAGE IN CAPITAL LETTERS.

Finally, use common sense. Before you send a message, ask yourself how you would feel if you received it.

Internet Issues

The Internet is very new. New Web sites are added daily, and the information on them changes constantly.

It is important to check the accuracy of your information. Is the source reliable? Is the information current? Compare the information on different Web sites. Use your best judgment to choose the most accurate information.

It is also important to cite any information you get from the Internet if you use it in your compositions. Your teacher can show you how to cite Internet references correctly. Several Web sites also demonstrate the correct method for using Internet citations.

Conclusion

The Internet is still quite new, so you'll need patience as you work through each of the exercises in this book. If you aren't able to access a particular Web site, don't worry. You can still find the information you need. Use a different search engine, click on a different link, or try again later.

Have fun on your Internet adventure!

Dave Sperling

How to Use This Program

BEGIN: `http://www.prenhall.com/sperling`

Components

There are two parts to this program:
1. *Dave Sperling's Internet Activity Workbook*
2. the companion Web site at `http://www.prenhall.com/sperling`*

Student Directions

In the first chapter, you will meet and begin corresponding with a key pal. Go to the **Key Pal Page** on the companion Web site and follow the directions to find a key pal. You will be writing to this person as you go through the chapters in this workbook. If your key pal stops writing to you, don't worry. You can always go back to the Key Pal Page to find another key pal.

The chapters in the book have a variety of activities:

- **Key Pal Interchange.** Exchange e-mail messages with your key pal, then write your key pal's responses in your workbook.
- **Other Activities.** Go to the companion Web site and select the appropriate chapter. Search the Web for information and write it in your workbook. Then participate in a:
  - *Group Discussion.* Share information with your classmates.
  - *Role Play.* Perform a skit based on your findings.
    or
  - *Writing Activity.* Write a composition based on the chapter's theme. (If you want to publish your writing on the Web, go to the link for Student Writing and follow the directions.)
- **Follow Up.** Each chapter also has a section for:
  - *New Vocabulary.* Choose five new words, find their definitions in an on-line dictionary, and record them in a vocabulary log in your workbook.
  - *Bulletin Board.* Post your thoughts in a Web-based discussion forum.
  - *URL Puzzle Clue.* Search the Web to find the answer to a trivia question.

At the end of the book, you can solve a **URL Puzzle**! Write the circled letter from each chapter's URL Puzzle Clue in the URL Puzzle on page 141 of your workbook. When you think you have solved the puzzle, go to the **URL Puzzle Page** on the companion Web site and follow the directions. If your answer is correct, you will gain access to a secret Web site!

Teacher Forum

Each chapter's Web page has a link to a **Teacher Forum**. On this bulletin board, teachers can post messages about the activities and share ideas with other teachers.

*You must have a computer with live Internet and World Wide Web access.

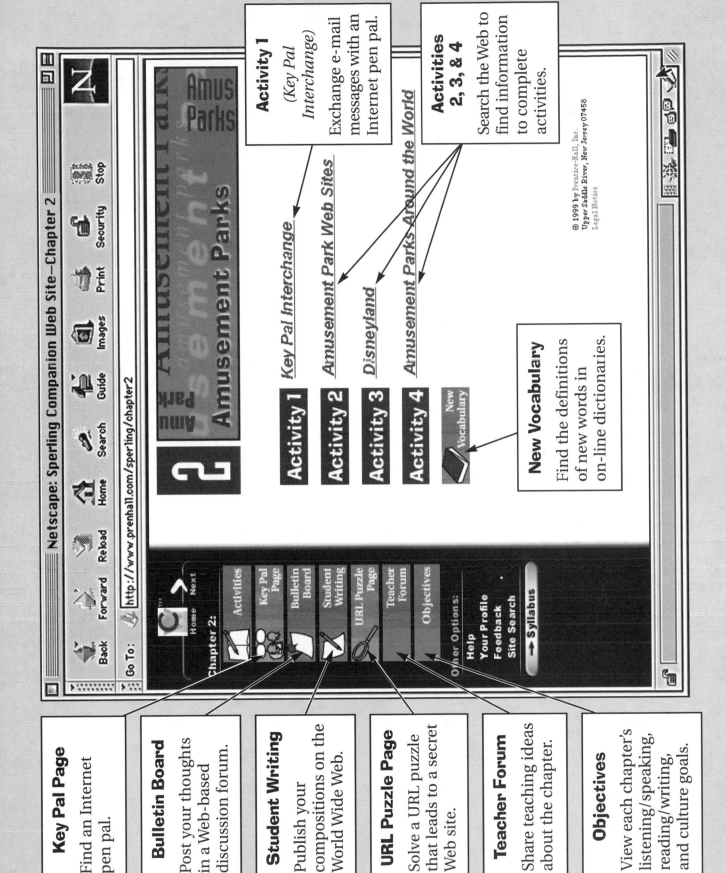

Key Pal Page
Find an Internet pen pal.

Bulletin Board
Post your thoughts in a Web-based discussion forum.

Student Writing
Publish your compositions on the World Wide Web.

URL Puzzle Page
Solve a URL puzzle that leads to a secret Web site.

Teacher Forum
Share teaching ideas about the chapter.

Objectives
View each chapter's listening/speaking, reading/writing, and culture goals.

Activity 1
(Key Pal Interchange)
Exchange e-mail messages with an Internet pen pal.

Activities 2, 3, & 4
Search the Web to find information to complete activities.

New Vocabulary
Find the definitions of new words in on-line dictionaries.

1 First Meeting

BEGIN: http://www.prenhall.com/sperling

> **❝ The only way to have a friend is to be one.❞**
>
> —*Ralph Waldo Emerson*

Activity 1

You and Your Key Pal

Directions: *Before you begin to search for a key pal, or Internet pen pal, write the following information about yourself in the spaces.*

Name	
E-mail address	
Country	
Sex	Age
Other information	

Directions: *Write the following information about your desired key pal in the spaces.*

Country	
Sex	Age range
Other information	

Group Discussion

Have you ever had a pen pal or key pal? Describe your experience. What criteria are important to you in a pen pal or key pal? Why? What criteria are not important? Why not?

Key Pal Search

Directions: *Go to the companion Web site and find the Key Pal Page. Follow the directions on the Web page to add your name to the list of key pals. Then follow the directions on the Web page to find a key pal. When you have finished, write the following information in the spaces.*

Number of key pals found _____

1. Name _____ Country _____

Sex ____ Age ____ E-mail address _____

2. Name _____ Country _____

Sex ____ Age ____ E-mail address _____

3. Name _____ Country _____

Sex ____ Age ____ E-mail address _____

4. Name _____ Country _____

Sex ____ Age ____ E-mail address _____

5. Name _____ Country _____

Sex ____ Age ____ E-mail address _____

6. Name _____ Country _____

Sex ____ Age ____ E-mail address _____

Group Discussion

Share your information with your group. How many key pals did you find? Which key pals interest you the most? Why?

Activity 3

Key Pal Introduction

Directions: *Write a short introduction about yourself in the space.*

Directions: *Choose a key pal from Activity 2. Send an e-mail message to the key pal. First, introduce yourself. Then ask the following questions. After your key pal answers, write information about him or her and his or her responses in the spaces. (**Note:** If your key pal does not respond within a few days, write to another person.)*

Information about Key Pal

Name _____ Country _____

Sex _____ Age _____ E-mail address _____

1. What do you do?

2. What do you look like?

3. What are your hobbies?

4. Describe your family.

5. Describe your hometown.

 Group Discussion

Describe your key pal to your group. How are you and your key pal similar? How are you different?

Key Pal Interview

Directions: *What else would you like to know about your key pal? Ask your key pal three more questions. Write your questions and your key pal's responses in the spaces.*

1.

2.

3.

Writing Activity

Write a paragraph or essay about your key pal.

FOLLOW UP

New Vocabulary

Write five new words you learned and their definitions.

1.

2.

3.

4.

5.

Amusement Parks

❝ It's kind of fun to do the impossible. ❞

—*Walt Disney*

Activity 1

Key Pal Interchange

Directions: *Ask your key pal the following questions. Then write the responses in the spaces.*

1. What amusement parks are popular in your country?

2. Why are they popular?

3. Have you ever been to an amusement park? If so, did you like it? Explain.

Directions: *Ask your key pal two more questions about amusement parks. Write your questions and your key pal's responses in the spaces.*

1.

2.

Group Discussion

Share your key pal's responses with your group.

Amusement Park Web Sites

Directions: *Search the Web for sites on amusement parks located in your country. Write down each site's name, URL, features, good points, and bad points. Check a rating for each site.*

1. Name of site

URL: http://

Features

Good points

Bad points

Rating ☐ Poor ☐ Fair ☐ Good ☐ Excellent

2. Name of site

URL: http://

Features

Good points

Bad points

Rating ☐ Poor ☐ Fair ☐ Good ☐ Excellent

3. Name of site

URL: http://

Features

Good points

Bad points

Rating ☐ Poor ☐ Fair ☐ Good ☐ Excellent

4. Name of site	
URL: http://	
Features	
Good points	
Bad points	

Rating ☐ Poor ☐ Fair ☐ Good ☐ Excellent

Writing Activity

Use the information you wrote down to write a review about one of the Web sites. First, describe the site. Then evaluate the site's good and bad points. Finally, tell your readers whether they should visit the site.

Activity 3

Disneyland

Directions: *Search the Web to find Disneyland's major attractions. Write the information in the spaces.*

Area	Attractions
1. Adventureland	The Enchanted Tiki Room, Indiana Jones Adventure, Jungle Cruise, and the Swiss Family Treehouse
2. Frontierland	
3. Fantasyland	
4. Tomorrowland	

Group Discussion

Which attractions do you think are the most fun? the most thrilling? Which attractions would you like to try? Why?

Amusement Parks Around the World

Directions: Search the Web to find information about amusement parks in the following countries. Write the information in the spaces.

1. France

Amusement park	Disneyland Paris
Address	Boite Postale 100, F-77777 Marne-la-Vallee, Cedex 4 France
Attractions	Main St. USA, Frontierland, Adventureland, Discoveryland, and Fantasyland

2. Japan

Amusement park	
Address	
Attractions	

3. Malaysia

Amusement park	
Address	
Attractions	

4. Another country

Amusement park	
Address	
Attractions	

5. Another country

Amusement park	
Address	
Attractions	

Group Discussion

Discuss what you like about the amusement parks. Then plan an amusement park for your city that will attract people of all ages from different countries. First, give it a name. Then decide on a location. Finally, decide on the attractions to include.

 FOLLOW UP

New Vocabulary

Write five new words you learned and their definitions.

1.

2.

3.

4.

5.

Bulletin Board

Post your thoughts about amusement parks on the Bulletin Board.

Chapter 2 URL Puzzle Clue

In what city is Disneyland located? Write the answer in the spaces. Then write the circled letter in the URL Puzzle on page 141.

☐ ☐ ☐ ☐ ◯ ☐

3

Animals

BEGIN: `http://www.prenhall.com/sperling`

> **"Cats are smarter than dogs. You can't get eight cats to pull a sled through snow."**
>
> —*Jeff Valdez*

Activity 1

Key Pal Interchange

Directions: *Ask your key pal the following questions. Then write the responses in the spaces.*

1. What's your favorite animal? Why?

2. Do you have any pets? If so, what are they? If not, would you like to have one?

3. Do you prefer cats or dogs? Why?

Directions: *Ask your key pal two more questions about animals. Write your questions and your key pal's responses in the spaces.*

1.

2.

Group Discussion

Share your key pal's responses with your group.

Animal Safari

Directions: *Search the Web to find information about the following animals. Write the information in the spaces.*

1. Chimpanzee

Description	They are 3'-5' tall and weigh 99-176 lbs. They have hairless faces, black hair, and no tails. Their arm span is 50% greater than their height.
Habitat	Humid forests, deciduous woods, and mixed savannahs in central & western Africa
Diet	Mainly fruit and young leaves.

2. Elephant

Description	
Habitat	
Diet	

3. Flamingo

Description	
Habitat	
Diet	

4. Iguana

Description	
Habitat	
Diet	

5. Another animal

Description	
Habitat	
Diet	

6. Another animal

Description	
Habitat	
Diet	

Group Discussion

Which animal looks the strangest? the scariest? the most beautiful? Which animal lives in the most unusual place? Which has the strangest diet? Explain your responses.

Activity 3

Extinct Animals

Directions: *Search the Web to find information about the following extinct animals. Write the information in the spaces.*

1. Spectacled Cormorant

Description — It was a plump bird large enough to feed 3-4 men at once. It was commonly found on Bering Island in the 1740's.

Date of extinction — 1852

Place of extinction — Bering Straits, Russia

Causes of extinction — It was hunted to extinction by sealers and hunters because it was slow and flightless.

2. Crescent Nailtail Wallaby

Description

Date of extinction

Place of extinction

Causes of extinction

3. Bourbon Crested Starling

Description

Date of extinction

Place of extinction

Causes of extinction

4. Laughing Owl

Description

Date of extinction

Place of extinction

Causes of extinction

Group Discussion

Why do you think these animals became extinct? Do you think any animals are in danger of becoming extinct today? If so, which ones? Why? Can we prevent animals from becoming extinct? If so, how?

Activity 4

Animal Sounds in English

Directions: Animal sounds are expressed differently in every language. Search the Web to find the English words for the sounds the following animals make. Write the words in the spaces.

Animal	Word	Animal	Word
1. Cat	*Meow*	**8.** Goose	
2. Chick		**9.** Hen	
3. Cow		**10.** Owl	
4. Cuckoo		**11.** Rooster	
5. Dog		**12.** Sheep	
6. Frog		**13.** Turkey	
7. Goat			

Writing Activity

Why do you think different languages express animal sounds differently? Write a paragraph in which you state and support your opinion.

FOLLOW UP

New Vocabulary

Write five new words you learned and their definitions.

1.	
2.	
3.	
4.	
5.	

Bulletin Board

Post your thoughts about animals on the Bulletin Board.

Chapter 3 URL Puzzle Clue

What is the name for a male kangaroo? Write the answer in the spaces. Then write the circled letter in the URL Puzzle on page 141.

☐ ☐ ◯ ☐ ☐ ☐

4 Architecture

BEGIN: http://www.prenhall.com/sperling

> **"Noble life demands a noble architecture for noble uses of noble men."**
>
> —*Frank Lloyd Wright*

Activity 1

Key Pal Interchange

Directions: *Ask your key pal the following questions. Then write the responses in the spaces.*

1. What is the tallest building in your city or town? How high is it?

2. What kind of architecture do you like? Why?

3. Are there any famous buildings or monuments in your city? If so, what are they?

Directions: *Ask your key pal two more questions about architecture. Write your questions and your key pal's responses in the spaces.*

1.

2.

Group Discussion

Share your key pal's responses with your group.

World's Tallest Buildings

Directions: *Search the Web to find information about the ten tallest buildings in the world. Write the information in the spaces.*

	Building	City	Stories	Feet
1.	Suyong Bay Tower	Pusan	88	1516
2.				
3.				
4.				
5.				
6.				
7.				
8.				
9.				
10.				

Group Discussion

Compare your answers. What city or town in your country has the tallest building? How many stories does it have? How tall is it?

New York City Skyscrapers

Directions: *Imagine that you're taking a trip to New York City. Search the Web to find information about a skyscraper in each of the following areas of the city. Write the information in the spaces.*

1. Park Avenue

Building name	The 101 Park Avenue Building
Address	101 Park Avenue at 40th Street
Description	It was built in 1985 as a 188.5m tall, 50-story, black, glass-steel building with a split-hexagon form.

2. Wall Street

Building name	
Address	
Description	

3. Times Square

Building name

Address

Description

4. Sixth Avenue

Building name

Address

Description

 Writing Activity

Write a paragraph or essay describing one of the skyscrapers.

Activity 4

Architecture Around the World

Directions: *Search the Web for information about a famous building or monument in each of the following countries. Write the information in the spaces.*

1. China

Name of building Beijing Institute of Architectural Design and Research

Location Beijing, China

Interesting facts It was built in 1949 for a design and research firm specializing in public, civil, and light industrial building.

2. Canada

Name of building

Location

Interesting facts

3. Italy

Name of building

Location

Interesting facts

4. Another country

Name of building

Location

Interesting facts

5. Another country	
Name of building	
Location	
Interesting facts	

Group Discussion

Share your information with your group. Then describe a famous building or monument in your country.

FOLLOW UP

New Vocabulary

Write five new words you learned and their definitions.

1.	
2.	
3.	
4.	
5.	

Bulletin Board

Post your thoughts about architecture on the Bulletin Board.

Chapter 4 URL Puzzle Clue

What pharaoh built the largest pyramid in the world? Write the answer in the spaces. Then write the circled letter in the URL Puzzle on page 141.

☐ ☐ Ⓞ ☐ ☐

 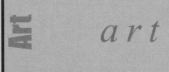 

5 Art

> **❝Art is the desire of a man to express himself, to record the reactions of his personality to the world he lives in.❞**
>
> —*Amy Lowell*

Activity 1

Key Pal Interchange

Directions: *Ask your key pal the following questions. Then write the responses in the spaces.*

1. Do you like to visit museums or art galleries? Explain.

2. What museums or art galleries have you visited? Describe one or two.

3. Who is the most famous artist in your country? Describe his or her art.

Directions: *Ask your key pal two more questions about art. Write your questions and your key pal's responses in the spaces.*

1.

2.

Group Discussion

Share your key pal's responses with your group.

Photo Search

Directions: *Visit on-line photo galleries and identify three photographs that interest you. Find the following information and write it in the spaces.*

1. Name of gallery

URL: http://

Photographer

Description of photo

2. Name of gallery

URL: http://

Photographer

Description of photo

3. Name of gallery

URL: http://

Photographer

Description of photo

 ## Writing Activity

Using one of the photos as a starting point, write a short story.

Activity 3

Famous Artists

Directions: *Search the Web for information about the following artists. Then write the information in the spaces.*

1. Frida Kahlo

| Date of birth | July 6, 1907 | Place of birth | Mexico |

Famous paintings: Between the Curtains, Roots, The Wounded Deer

Facts about the artist: She went from a legend, to a myth, to a cult figure. Her work was autobiographical and depicted her personal sagas.

2. Rembrandt van Rijn

Date of birth [ ] Place of birth [ ]

Famous paintings [ ]

Facts about the artist [ ]

3. Xu Beihong

Date of birth [ ] Place of birth [ ]

Famous paintings [ ]

Facts about the artist [ ]

4. Another artist [ ]

Date of birth [ ] Place of birth [ ]

Famous paintings [ ]

Facts about the artist [ ]

5. Another artist [ ]

Date of birth [ ] Place of birth [ ]

Famous paintings [ ]

Facts about the artist [ ]

 Group Discussion

Share your information with your group. Which artist's work do you like the best? Why? Which artist do you think had the most unusual life? Why?

Activity 4

A Visit to the Louvre Museum

Directions: *Search the Web to find different works of art at the Louvre Museum in Paris. Choose three paintings, sculptures, or other works of art. Write down the name of each work, the artist, and the completion date. Then describe the work.*

1. Work of art [ ]

Artist [ ] Date [ ]

Description [ ]

2. Work of art	
Artist	Date
Description	

3. Work of art	
Artist	Date
Description	

Writing Activity

Imagine that you are an art critic. Write a review of one of the three works of art. First, state the name of the work, the artist, and the completion date. Then describe the work. Finally, give your opinion about it.

FOLLOW UP

New Vocabulary

Write five new words you learned and their definitions.

1.

2.

3.

4.

5.

Bulletin Board

Post your thoughts about art on the Bulletin Board.

Chapter 5 URL Puzzle Clue

What artist painted the Mona Lisa? Write the answer in the spaces. Then write the circled letter in the URL Puzzle on page 141.

☐ ☐ ☐ ☐ ☐ ☐ ☐ ☐ ◯ ☐ ☐ ☐ ☐ ☐

6 Astrology

astrology

BEGIN: http://www.prenhall.com/sperling

> **66 Before a war, military science seems a real science, like astronomy. After a war it seems more like astrology."**
>
> —*Dame Rebecca West*

Activity 1

Key Pal Interchange

Directions: *Ask your key pal the following questions. Then write the responses in the spaces.*

1. Do you know your astrological sign? If so, what is it?

2. Do you believe in astrology? Explain.

Directions: *Ask your key pal two more questions about astrology. Write your questions and your key pal's responses in the spaces.*

1.

2.

Group Discussion

Share your key pal's responses with your group.

Astrological Search

Directions: *Search the Web for the dates and personality traits for the following astrological signs. Write the information in the spaces.*

Sign	Dates	Personality Traits
1. Aries	3/21 to 4/19	independent, self-assertive, and active
2. Taurus		
3. Gemini		
4. Cancer		
5. Leo		
6. Virgo		
7. Libra		
8. Scorpio		
9. Sagittarius		
10. Capricorn		
11. Aquarius		
12. Pisces		

Group Discussion

What's your sign? Do you think your personality traits match the personality traits for your sign? Why or why not?

Activity 3

Daily Horoscope

Directions: *Search the Web to find your horoscope for today. Write the information in the space.*

Writing Activity

Compare your day to the prediction in your horoscope. Write a paragraph explaining whether you think your horoscope is accurate.

Activity 4

Chinese Astrology

Directions: *According to Chinese astrology, the animal that rules your lunar year of birth determines your personality. For example, if you were born in the year of the Rat, you would have personality traits similar to those of the rat. Search the Web to find the lunar years and the personality traits for each animal. Then find celebrities who were born in those years. Write the information in the spaces.*

1. Rat
Lunar years	1900, 1912, 1924, 1936, 1948, 1960, 1972, 1984, 1996
Personality traits	charming, aggressive, and expressive
Celebrities	Plato, Mozart, Tolstoy

2. Ox
Lunar years	
Personality traits	
Celebrities	

3. Tiger
Lunar years	
Personality traits	
Celebrities	

4. Rabbit
Lunar years	
Personality traits	
Celebrities	

5. Dragon

    Lunar years

    Personality traits

    Celebrities

6. Snake

    Lunar years

    Personality traits

    Celebrities

7. Horse

    Lunar years

    Personality traits

    Celebrities

8. Goat

    Lunar years

    Personality traits

    Celebrities

9. Monkey

    Lunar years

    Personality traits

    Celebrities

10. Rooster

    Lunar years

    Personality traits

    Celebrities

11. Dog

    Lunar years

    Personality traits

    Celebrities

12. Pig

    Lunar years

    Personality traits

    Celebrities

Group Discussion

Which animal rules your year of birth? Do you think your personality traits match the personality traits for that animal? Why or why not? Do you think the celebrities' personality traits match the personality traits for the animals associated with their signs? Why or why not? Does your culture attribute to animals the same personality traits as does Chinese astrology? If not, how are the traits different?

FOLLOW UP

New Vocabulary

Write five new words you learned and their definitions.

1.

2.

3.

4.

5.

Bulletin Board

Post your thoughts about astrology on the Bulletin Board.

Chapter 6 URL Puzzle Clue

Which astrological sign is symbolized by a centaur with a bow? Write the answer in the spaces. Then write the circled letter in the URL Puzzle on page 141.

☐ ☐ ◯ ☐ ☐ ☐ ☐ ☐ ☐ ☐ ☐

7 Cities

BEGIN: http://www.prenhall.com/sperling

"The city is not a concrete jungle, it is a human zoo."

—*Desmond Morris*

Activity 1

Key Pal Interchange

Directions: *Ask your key pal the following questions. Then write the responses in the spaces.*

1. What is the largest city in your country?

2. Do you prefer to live in the city or in the countryside? Why?

3. What are some advantages to living in the city? some disadvantages?

4. What are some advantages to living in the countryside? some disadvantages?

Directions: *Ask your key pal two more questions about cities. Write your questions and your key pal's responses in the spaces.*

1.

2.

Group Discussion

Share your key pal's responses with your group.

City Web Sites

Directions: *Search the Web for sites on your city. Write down each site's name, URL, features, good points, and bad points. Check a rating for each site.*

1. Name of site

URL: http://

Features

Good points

Bad points

Rating ☐ Poor ☐ Fair ☐ Good ☐ Excellent

2. Name of site

URL: http://

Features

Good points

Bad points

Rating ☐ Poor ☐ Fair ☐ Good ☐ Excellent

3. Name of site

URL: http://

Features

Good points

Bad points

Rating ☐ Poor ☐ Fair ☐ Good ☐ Excellent

4. Name of site	
URL: http://	
Features	
Good points	
Bad points	
Rating	☐ Poor ☐ Fair ☐ Good ☐ Excellent

Writing Activity

Use the information you wrote down to write a review about one of the Web sites. First, describe the site. Then evaluate the site's good and bad points. Finally, tell your readers whether they should visit the site.

Activity 3

Population Density

Directions: *Search the Web for population and area information for Los Angeles, Tokyo, Nairobi, your city, and two other cities. Write the information in the spaces.*

1. Los Angeles		**4.** Your city	
Population		Population	
Area		Area	
2. Nairobi		**5.** Another city	
Population		Population	
Area		Area	
3. Tokyo		**6.** Another city	
Population		Population	
Area		Area	

Group Discussion

Population density is "the number of people per square mile or kilometer." For example, if 50 people live in 1 square mile, the population density is 50 people per square mile. Calculate the population densities for the cities listed above. Which city has the highest population density? the lowest population density? Which of these cities do you think are too crowded? Explain.

Activity 4

Distances Between Cities

Directions: *Search the Web to find the distances (in miles or kilometers) between the cities. Write the information in the spaces.*

Cities			Distance
1. Tokyo, Japan	to	Los Angeles, California	5478 miles
2. Sydney, Australia	to	Paris, France	
3. New York City, New York	to	Santiago, Chile	
4. Bangkok, Thailand	to	Tel Aviv, Israel	
5. Cairo, Egypt	to	Nairobi, Kenya	
6. London, England	to	Madrid, Spain	
Other Cities			
7.	to		
8.	to		

Group Discussion

Discuss your answers with your group. Which two cities are the closest together? the farthest apart?

Activity 5

Visitor Information

Directions: *Choose three cities that you would like to visit. Search the Web to find the following information. Write it in the spaces.*

1. City of your choice	
When to go	
What to pack	
What to eat	
What to do	
Where to stay	
How to get around	
Safety information	
Other information	

2. Another city

When to go	
What to pack	
What to eat	
What to do	
Where to stay	
How to get around	
Safety information	
Other information	

3. Another city

When to go	
What to pack	
What to eat	
What to do	
Where to stay	
How to get around	
Safety information	
Other information	

Writing Activity

Choose one city and write a travel brochure to promote it.

FOLLOW UP

New Vocabulary

Write five new words you learned and their definitions.

1.

2.

3.

4.

5.

Bulletin Board

Post your thoughts about cities on the Bulletin Board.

Chapter 7 URL Puzzle Clue

What is the former name for Jakarta? Write the answer in the spaces. Then write the circled letter in the URL Puzzle on page 141.

8 Countries

"How do you govern a country which has 246 different kinds of cheese?"

—*Charles De Gaulle*

Activity 1

Key Pal Interchange

Directions: *Ask your key pal the following questions. Then write the responses in the spaces.*

1. What countries have you visited? Which did you like the best? Why?

2. What country would you like to visit? Why?

3. What countries border your country?

Directions: *Ask your key pal two more questions about countries. Write your questions and your key pal's responses in the spaces.*

1.

2.

Group Discussion

Share your key pal's responses with your group.

The United Nations

Directions: *The United Nations consists of many different organizations, which are often called by their abbreviations. For example, the United Nations is often called the UN. The abbreviations for five UN organizations are listed below. Search the Web to find each organization's complete name, headquarters, year founded, and purpose. Write the information in the spaces.*

1. UNCHS

Complete name	United Nations Center for Human Settlements
Headquarters	Nairobi, Kenya
Year founded	1978
Purpose	It is the lead agency for the UN's human settlement development activities and for exchange of information on human settlement trends.

2. UNEP

Complete name	
Headquarters	
Year founded	
Purpose	

3. UNICEF

Complete name	
Headquarters	
Year founded	
Purpose	

4. WFP

Complete name	
Headquarters	
Year founded	
Purpose	

5. WHO

Complete name	
Headquarters	
Year founded	
Purpose	

Writing Activity

Choose one of the above organizations. Do you think it is achieving its purpose? Support your opinion in a paragraph or essay.

Activity 3

Countries of the World

Directions: *Choose six countries that interest you. Search the Web for the following information and write it in the spaces.*

1. Country _____
Area _____
Capital _____
Largest city _____
Languages _____
Population _____

2. Country _____
Area _____
Capital _____
Largest city _____
Languages _____
Population _____

3. Country _____
Area _____
Capital _____
Largest city _____
Languages _____
Population _____

4. Country _____
Area _____
Capital _____
Largest city _____
Languages _____
Population _____

5. Country	
Area	
Capital	
Largest city	
Languages	
Population	
6. Country	
Area	
Capital	
Largest city	
Languages	
Population	

Writing Activity

Which country would you most like to visit? Why? Explain your reasons in a paragraph or essay.

Activity 4

World Time

Directions: *Search the Web to find the current time for each of the following locations. Then write the information in the spaces.*

Location	Time	Location	Time
1. London, England		**6.** Tokyo, Japan	
2. Madrid, Spain		**7.** Nairobi, Kenya	
3. Damascus, Syria		**8.** Ontario, Canada	
4. Oregon, USA		**9.** New York, USA	
5. Bogota, Colombia		**10.** Honolulu, Hawaii	

Group Discussion

Which locations are in the same time zone as yours? Which locations are ahead of yours? Which locations are behind yours? Are there any locations that are a day ahead or a day behind where you live? If so, which ones?

New Vocabulary

Write five new words you learned and their definitions.

1.

2.

3.

4.

5.

Bulletin Board

Post your thoughts about countries on the Bulletin Board.

Chapter 8 URL Puzzle Clue

Which country used to be called Taprobane? Write the answer in the spaces. Then write the circled letter in the URL Puzzle on page 141.

☐ ☐ ☐ ◯ ☐ ☐ ☐

Crime
Crime
Crime

BEGIN: `http://www.prenhall.com/sperling`

> **"Commit a crime and the earth is made of glass."**
>
> —*Ralph Waldo Emerson*

Activity 1

Key Pal Interchange

Directions: Ask your key pal the following questions. Then write the responses in the spaces.

1. Is your city considered safe or dangerous? Explain?

2. What kinds of crime are common in your country?

3. Are there any notorious criminals in your country? If so, name one and describe his or her crimes.

Directions: Ask your key pal two more questions about crime or criminals. Write your questions and your key pal's responses in the spaces.

1.

2.

Group Discussion

Share your key pal's responses with your group.

Infamous American Criminals

Directions: *Search the Web to find information about the following infamous American criminals. Write the information in the spaces.*

1. Billy the Kid

Date of birth — Unknown

Crimes — He killed many, including Sheriff Bill Brady.

Interesting facts — He was the most famous outlaw and gunfighter in the Southwest frontier. He played a leading role in the Lincoln County War. Real name: William Bonney.

2. John Dillinger

Date of birth

Crimes

Interesting facts

3. Al Capone

Date of birth

Crimes

Interesting facts

4. Jesse James

Date of birth

Crimes

Interesting facts

5. Another criminal

Date of birth

Crimes

Interesting facts

Writing Activity

Choose one of the criminals listed. Write a paragraph or essay describing one of his or her crimes. Include as many interesting details as possible.

The FBI's Ten Most Wanted Fugitives

Directions: *Search the Web to find the FBI's (Federal Bureau of Investigation's) ten most wanted fugitives. Then write down each fugitive's name, crime, and the reward offered.*

1. Name

Crime

Reward

2. Name

Crime

Reward

3. Name

Crime

Reward

4. Name

Crime

Reward

5. Name

Crime

Reward

6. Name

Crime

Reward

7. Name

Crime

Reward

8. Name

Crime

Reward

9. Name

Crime

Reward

10. Name	
Crime	
Reward	

Group Discussion

Which criminal do you think is the most dangerous? Why? Rank the fugitives from the most dangerous (1) to the least dangerous (10).

Activity 4

Types of Crime

Directions: Search the Web to find the definition for each crime. Write the information in the spaces.

Crime	Definition
1. Homicide	The killing of one human being by another human being
2. Fraud	
3. Kidnapping	
4. Burglary	
5. Treason	

Group Discussion

Are any of these crimes common in your country? If so, which ones? What are the penalties? Do you think that stronger penalties help prevent crime? Why or why not?

FOLLOW UP

New Vocabulary

Write five new words you learned and their definitions.

1.
2.

3.

4.

5.

Bulletin Board

Post your thoughts about crime on the Bulletin Board.

Chapter 9 URL Puzzle Clue

What human rights organization won the Nobel Peace Prize in 1977? Write the answer in the spaces. Then write the circled letter in the URL Puzzle on page 141.

☐ ☐ ☐ ☐ ☐ ☐ ☐

☐ ☐ ☐ ☐ ☐ ☐ ☐ ☐ ☐ ☐ ☐ ☐ ☐

BEGIN: `http://www.prenhall.com/sperling`

"I want the cultures of all the lands to be blown about my house as freely as possible."

—*Mahatma Gandhi*

Activity 1

Key Pal Interchange

Directions: *Ask your key pal the following questions. Then write the responses in the spaces.*

1. What information should I know about your country before I visit it?

2. What special ceremonies are celebrated in your country? Briefly describe one or two.

Directions: *Ask your key pal two more questions about his or her country's culture. Write your questions and your key pal's responses in the spaces.*

1.

2.

Group Discussion

Share your key pal's responses with your group.

Proverb Search

Directions: *A proverb is "a short saying that expresses a truth." Search the Web for proverbs from around the world. Write the information in the spaces.*

1. Your country

Proverb

2. Another country

Proverb

3. Another country

Proverb

4. Another country

Proverb

5. Another country

Proverb

Group Discussion

Discuss each proverb. What do you think it means? Are there any similar proverbs from your country? If so, what are they?

World Folk Tales

Directions: *A folk tale is "a story that is passed down from generation to generation." Search the Web to find a folk tale. Write down the name of the folk tale and its origin. After you read the folk tale, write the names of the main characters and a summary of the folk tale.*

Name of folk tale	
Origin	
Characters	
Summary	

Role Play

Write a skit about the folk tale. Then assign roles and practice the skit. Finally perform it for your class.

Gestures

Directions: *A gesture is "a movement of the body or limbs that expresses an idea or feeling." Search the Web to find gestures from the countries listed below. Describe each gesture and write its meaning in the spaces.*

1. Malaysia

Gesture — standing with your hands on your hips

Meaning — a sign of anger

2. Brazil

Gesture

Meaning

3. Greece

Gesture

Meaning

4. Kenya

Gesture

Meaning

5. Another country

Gesture

Meaning

6. Another country

Gesture

Meaning

Group Discussion

Do these gestures have the same meanings in your country? If not, what do they mean? Are there any special gestures from your country? If so, demonstrate them and explain what they mean.

Countercultures

Directions: *A counterculture is "a culture with lifestyles and attitudes opposed to those of the established culture." Search the Web to find a definition for each of the following American countercultures. Write the information in the spaces.*

Counterculture	Definition
1. Beat generation	
2. Cyber-culture	
3. Generation X	
4. Hippies	
5. New age	

Writing Activity

Write a paragraph or essay about a past or present culture or counterculture in your country.

 **FOLLOW UP**

New Vocabulary

Write five new words you learned and their definitions.

1.	
2.	
3.	

4.

5.

Bulletin Board

Post your thoughts about culture on the Bulletin Board.

Chapter 10 URL Puzzle Clue

What is the word for "a portable conical dwelling used by Native American peoples"? Write the answer in the spaces. Then write the circled letter in the URL Puzzle on page 141.

11 Education

"Experience is a good school, but the fees are high."

— *Heinrich Heine*

Activity 1

Key Pal Interchange

Directions: *Ask your key pal the following questions. Then write the responses in the spaces.*

1. What is (or was) your favorite subject? Why?

2. Have you ever taken any special classes after school? If so, what are (or were) they?

3. What is the most famous college or university in your country? Where is it located?

Directions: *Ask your key pal two more questions about education. Write your questions and your key pal's responses in the spaces.*

1.

2.

Group Discussion

Share your key pal's responses with your group.

Specialized Schools

Directions: *Search the Web for definitions of the following types of specialized schools. Write the information in the spaces.*

1. Boarding school

> A school at which students receive meals and housing.

2. Charter school

3. College preparatory school

4. Home school

5. Magnet school

6. Montessori school

7. Ski academy

8. Waldorf school

 ## Group Discussion

Share your information with your group. Do any of these specialized schools exist in your country? If so, which ones? Do other specialized schools exist in your country? If so, describe them.

Continuing Education

Directions: *Continuing education courses are designed for part-time adult students. Search the Web to find three schools that offer continuing education courses. Write the information in the spaces on the following page.*

1. Name of school	
Location	
URL: http://	
Courses	

2. Name of school	
Location	
URL: http://	
Courses	

3. Name of school	
Location	
URL: http://	
Courses	

 ## Writing Activity

Which continuing education course would you most like to study? Why? Explain your reasons in a paragraph or essay.

Activity 4

The Five Top-Rated American Universities

Directions: *Search the Web for information about the five top-rated universities in the United States. Write the information in the spaces.*

1. Name of university			
Private/Public school		Number of students	
Year founded		Setting	
Religious affiliation		Tuition and fees	
2. Name of university			
Private/Public school		Number of students	
Year founded		Setting	
Religious affiliation		Tuition and fees	

3. Name of university

Private/Public school		Number of students	
Year founded		Setting	
Religious affiliation		Tuition and fees	

4. Name of university

Private/Public school		Number of students	
Year founded		Setting	
Religious affiliation		Tuition and fees	

5. Name of university

Private/Public school		Number of students	
Year founded		Setting	
Religious affiliation		Tuition and fees	

Group Discussion

Compare the five top-rated universities in the United States with the five top-rated universities in your country. How are they similar? How are they different? Do you think it is more difficult to enter a university in the United States or a university in your country? Explain.

FOLLOW UP

New Vocabulary

Write five new words you learned and their definitions.

1.

2.

3.

4.

5.

Bulletin Board

Post your thoughts about education on the Bulletin Board.

Chapter 11 URL Puzzle Clue

What is the word for "a European secondary school that prepares students for university"? Write the answer in the spaces. Then write the circled letter in the URL Puzzle on page 141.

☐ ☐ ☐ ☐ ☐ ☐ ◯ ☐ ☐

12 Family and Marriage

> **"Compromise, if not the spice of life, is its solidity. It is what makes nations great and marriages happy."**
>
> — *Phyllis McGinley*

Activity 1

Key Pal Interchange

Directions: *Ask your key pal the following questions. Then write the responses in the spaces.*

1. How many brothers and sisters do you have? Describe them.

2. Describe a wedding ceremony in your country.

Directions: *Ask your key pal two more questions about family and marriage. Write your questions and your key pal's responses in the spaces.*

1.

2.

Group Discussion

Share your key pal's responses with your group.

Family Home Page

Directions: Search the Web for a family's home page. Find the following information and write it in the spaces.

Family name	
URL: http://	
City	Country

Name of Family Member	Information about Person
1.	
2.	
3.	
4.	

Links to other Web pages:	

Group Discussion

Share your information with your group. Which family member would you most like to meet? Why? Are there any outside links from the family's home page? If so, what do they reveal about the family's interests?

Wedding Customs Around the World

Directions: Choose three countries. Search the Web to find a wedding custom in each country. Write the information in the spaces.

1. Country	
Wedding custom	

2. Country	
Wedding custom	

3. Country	
Wedding custom	

Writing Activity

Write a paragraph or essay about a wedding custom in your country.

Activity 4

Wedding Home Page

Directions: *Search the Web for a wedding home page. Find the following information and write it in the spaces.*

Bride's name	
Groom's name	
Wedding date	Wedding location
Features of wedding	

Group Discussion

Share your information with your group. Which features of the wedding do you like? If you are single, would you like to have a wedding like the one described? Why or why not? If you are married, describe your wedding. Would you like to create a home page about your wedding? Why or why not?

New Vocabulary

Write five new words you learned and their definitions.

1.

2.

3.

4.

5.

Bulletin Board

Post your thoughts about family and marriage on the Bulletin Board.

Chapter 12 URL Puzzle Clue

What is the word for "a head cover, such as that worn by a bride"? Write the answer in the spaces. Then write the circled letter in the URL Puzzle on page 141.

13 Food

BEGIN: `http://www.prenhall.com/sperling`

> **"Part of the secret of success in life is to eat what you like and let the food fight it out inside."**
>
> — *Mark Twain*

Activity 1

Key Pal Interchange

Directions: *Ask your key pal the following questions. Then write the responses in the spaces.*

1. What are your favorite foods?

2. What do you usually eat for breakfast? for lunch? for dinner?

3. Can you cook? If so, what can you make?

Directions: *Ask your key pal two more questions about food. Write your questions and your key pal's responses in the spaces.*

1.

2.

Group Discussion

Share your key pal's responses with your group.

Favorite Food Search

Directions: *Search the Web for information about your favorite food. Write the information in the spaces.*

1. Name of site

URL: http://

Information about food

2. Name of site

URL: http://

Information about food

3. Name of site

URL: http://

Information about food

Group Discussion

Share your information with your group. What did you already know about your favorite food? What did you learn?

International Recipes

Directions: *Choose three countries. Search the Web to find a recipe for a dish from each country. Write the information in the spaces.*

1. Dish

Country

Recipe

2. Dish

Country

Recipe

3. Dish

Country

Recipe

Writing Activity

Write a recipe for a popular dish from your country.

Restaurant Review

Directions: *Choose one American city that you would like to visit. Search the Web for information about three restaurants in that city. Write the information in the spaces.*

1. Name of restaurant

Address

Cuisine

Phone number   What to wear

Price for lunch   Price for dinner

Other information

2. Name of restaurant

Address

Cuisine

Phone number   What to wear

Price for lunch   Price for dinner

Other information

3. Name of restaurant

Address

Cuisine

Phone number   What to wear

Price for lunch   Price for dinner

Other information

Group Discussion

Share your information with your group. At which restaurant would you prefer to eat? Why?

New Vocabulary

Write five new words you learned and their definitions.

1.

2.

3.

4.

5.

 Bulletin Board

Post your thoughts about food on the Bulletin Board.

 Chapter 13 URL Puzzle Clue

What is the word for "a Japanese dish of battered, deep-fried seafood or vegetables"? Write the answer in the spaces. Then write the circled letter in the URL Puzzle on page 141.

☐ ☐ ☐ ☐ ☐ ☐ ☐

Games

BEGIN: http://www.prenhall.com/sperling

> **"If life doesn't offer a game worth playing, then invent a new one."**
>
> — *Anthony J. D'Angelo*

Activity 1

 Key Pal Interchange

Directions: *Ask your key pal the following questions. Then write the responses in the spaces.*

1. What is your favorite game? Why?

2. What games are popular in your country?

Directions: *Ask your key pal two more questions about games. Write your questions and your key pal's responses in the spaces.*

1.

2.

 Group Discussion

Share your key pal's responses with your group.

Game Search

Directions: *Search the Web to find games for each of the following categories. Write the names of the games in the spaces.*

1. Board games

Chess,

4. Internet games

Cyberhunt,

2. Card games

Blackjack,

5. Role playing games

Conspiracy X,

3. Computer games

Myst,

6. Video games

Mortal Kombat,

Group Discussion

Share your information with your group. Which of these games have you played? Which do you like? Why? Which do you dislike? Why?

Activity 3

Computer Game Search

Directions: *Search the Web to find information about three different computer games. Write the information in the spaces.*

1. Name of game

URL: http://

Description

2. Name of game

URL: http://

Description

3. Name of game

URL: http://

Description

Writing Activity

Do you think computer games are a good use of time? Why or why not? Explain your reasons in a paragraph or essay.

On-line Games

Directions: *Play an on-line game with your key pal. After you have finished, write the following information in the spaces.*

Name of game		
Description of game		
Date played	Winner	
Technical problems		
Solutions		

Group Discussion

Share your experience with your group. Did you have any technical problems while playing the game? If so, what were they? Were you able to solve them? Did you enjoy the game? Why or why not? Would you play an on-line game again? Why or why not?

New Vocabulary

Write five new words you learned and their definitions.

1.

2.

3.

4.

5.

Bulletin Board

Post your thoughts about games on the Bulletin Board.

Chapter 14 URL Puzzle Clue

What game of Chinese origin was originally played with 136 or 144 tiles? Write the answer in the spaces. Then write the circled letter in the URL Puzzle on page 141.

☐ ☐ ☐ ☐ ◯ ☐ ☐

15 geography
Geography

❝ boundary, n. In political geography, an imaginary line between two nations, separating the imaginary rights of one from the imaginary rights of the other.**❞**

— *Ambrose Bierce,* The Devil's Dictionary

Activity 1

Key Pal Interchange

Directions: *Ask your key pal the following questions. Then write the responses in the spaces.*

1. What is the highest mountain in your country? Where is it?

2. What is the longest river in your country? Where is it?

Directions: *Ask your key pal two more questions about the geography in his or her country. Write your questions and your key pal's responses in the spaces.*

1.

2.

Group Discussion

Share your key pal's responses with your group.

Explorer Search

Directions: *Search the Web for information about each of the following explorers.*
Write the information in the spaces.

1. Amerigo Vespucci

Date of birth   March 9, 1454

Birthplace   Florence, Italy

Explorations   He explored the coast of South America and identified the New World of North and South America as separate from Asia.

2. Captain James Cook

Date of birth

Birthplace

Explorations

3. Marco Polo

Date of birth

Birthplace

Explorations

4. Another explorer

Date of birth

Birthplace

Explorations

5. Another explorer

Date of birth

Birthplace

Explorations

Group Discussion

Share your information with your group. Which of these explorations most interests you? Why? Would you like to be an explorer? If so, where would you like to go? If not, why not?

Activity 3

Top of the World

Directions: *Where are the world's highest mountains, largest lakes, largest islands, and longest rivers? Search the Web for the following information and write it in the spaces.*

1. The world's three highest mountains

	Name	Location	Height
a.			
b.			
c.			

2. The world's three largest lakes

	Name	Location	Area
a.			
b.			
c.			

3. The world's three largest islands

	Name	Location	Area
a.			
b.			
c.			

4. The world's three longest rivers

	Name	Source	Length
a.			
b.			
c.			

 Writing Activity

Write a paragraph or essay describing a famous mountain, lake, island, or river in your country.

On-line Geography Game

Directions: *Play an on-line geography game. After you have finished, write the following information in the spaces.*

Name of game	
Level (if any)	
Description of game	
Score	

 ### Group Discussion

Share your experience with your group. Did you enjoy the game? Why or why not? Were you satisfied with your score? If not, what can you do to improve it?

FOLLOW UP

 ### New Vocabulary

Write five new words you learned and their definitions.

1.	
2.	
3.	
4.	
5.	

 ### Bulletin Board

Post your thoughts about geography on the Bulletin Board.

Chapter 15 URL Puzzle Clue

What is the name of the world's highest waterfall? Write the answer in the spaces. Then write the circled letter in the URL Puzzle on page 141.

□ □ □ □ □ □ □ □ □ ◯

16 Health

"A man too busy to take care of his health is like a mechanic too busy to take care of his tools."

— *Spanish proverb*

Activity 1

Key Pal Interchange

Directions: *Ask your key pal the following questions. Then write the responses in the spaces.*

1. Do you exercise? If so, what kind of exercise do you do?

2. What foods do you think are healthy? Why?

3. What foods do you think are unhealthy? Why?

Directions: *Ask your key pal two more questions about health. Write your questions and your key pal's responses in the spaces.*

1.

2.

Group Discussion

Share your key pal's responses with your group.

The Food Guide Pyramid

Directions: *Search the Web to find the U.S. Department of Agriculture Food Guide Pyramid. Write the recommended number of servings per day and examples of each food group in the spaces.*

Food Group	Number of Servings	Examples of Foods
1. Fats, oils, & sweets	use sparingly	butter, margarine, gravy, soft drinks, salad dressing, candy, sugar, and jelly
2. Milk, yogurt, & cheese		
3. Meat, poultry, fish, eggs, & nuts		
4. Fruit		
5. Vegetable		
6. Bread, cereal, rice, & pasta		

Group Discussion

Tell your group about your daily diet. Do you think you should improve your diet? If so, how?

Activity 3

Ailments and Their Causes

Directions: *Search the Web to find causes for the following ailments. Write the information in the spaces.*

Ailment	Cause
1. Asthma	Usually a result of genetics, but can develop in anyone through an allergic reaction.
2. Cancer	
3. Diabetes	
4. Heart attack	

5. Lung cancer	
6. Stroke	
7. Another ailment	
8. Another ailment	

Group Discussion

Share your answers with your group. Do you think any of these ailments can be prevented? If so, how?

Exercise and Health Benefits

Directions: Search the Web to find the health benefits of the following types of exercise. Write the information in the spaces.

Exercise	Health Benefits
1. Cycling	reduced risk of heart disease, high blood pressure, stroke, and death
2. Running	
3. Swimming	
4. Tennis	
5. Walking	
6. Yoga	
7. Another exercise	
8. Another exercise	

Writing Activity

Write a paragraph or essay about your favorite type of exercise.

FOLLOW UP

New Vocabulary

Write five new words you learned and their definitions.

1.
2.
3.
4.
5.

Bulletin Board

Post your thoughts about exercise on the Bulletin Board.

Chapter 16 URL Puzzle Clue

What United Nations agency is concerned with improving health? Write the answer in the spaces. Then write the circled letter in the URL Puzzle on page 141.

☐ ◯ ☐ ☐ ☐   ☐ ☐ ☐ ☐ ☐

☐ ☐ ☐ ☐ ☐ ☐ ☐ ☐ ☐ ☐ ☐ ☐

BEGIN: `http://www.prenhall.com/sperling`

> **"History will be kind to me for I intend to write it."**
>
> —*Winston Churchill*

Activity 1

Key Pal Interchange

Directions: *Ask your key pal the following questions. Then write the responses in the spaces.*

1. Describe a famous event in your country's history.

2. Who is your favorite historical figure? Why?

Directions: *Ask your key pal two more questions about history. Write your questions and your key pal's responses in the spaces.*

1.

2.

Group Discussion

Share your key pal's responses with your group.

This Day in History

Directions: Search the Web to find an important event that occurred on this day in history. Write the information in the spaces.

Today's date	
Date in history	
Event	

Role Play

Write a skit about the historical event. Then assign roles and practice the skit. Finally, perform it for your class.

Chinese Dynasties

Directions: Search the Web to find information about the following Chinese dynasties, or periods of rule. Write the information in the spaces.

1. Zhou Dynasty   Dates   1111 to 222 B.C.

Events   *A dynasty during the classical age when there was much political disorder. King Wen laid down the foundation for the dynasty by setting out to destroy the Shang Dynasty.*

2. Sui Dynasty   Dates

Events

3. Tang Dynasty   Dates

Events

4. Ming Dynasty   Dates

Events

5. Qing Dynasty   Dates

Events

Group Discussion

Share your information with your group. Then describe a significant era in your country's history. Include as many important events as possible.

Activity 4

Historical Events in the United States

Directions: *Search the Web to find information about the following historical events in the United States. Write the information in the spaces.*

1. The Statue of Liberty was unveiled in New York Harbor.

Date   October 28, 1886

Information   The Statue is a 225-ton, steel-reinforced copper, female figure. It is 152' tall, and it commemorates the alliance of France with the American colonies during the American Revolution.

2. The Supreme Court ruled that segregation was illegal.

Date

Information

3. John F. Kennedy was elected President.

Date

Information

4. The civil rights leader Martin Luther King, Jr., was assassinated.

Date

Information

5. The United States withdrew troops from Vietnam.

Date

Information

6. Congress passed the Americans with Disabilities Act.

Date

Information

Writing Activity

Choose one of the historical events. Write a paragraph or essay describing the event.

FOLLOW UP

New Vocabulary

Write five new words you learned and their definitions.

1.

2.

3.

4.

5.

Bulletin Board

Post your thoughts about history on the Bulletin Board.

Chapter 17 URL Puzzle Clue

In what city was Christopher Columbus born? Write the answer in the spaces. Then write the circled letter in the URL Puzzle on page 141.

18 Holidays

BEGIN: `http://www.prenhall.com/sperling`

> **❝If all the year were playing holidays, to sport would be as tedious as to work.❞**
>
> —*William Shakespeare*

Activity 1

Key Pal Interchange

Directions: *Ask your key pal the following questions. Then write the responses in the spaces.*

1. What is the most popular holiday in your country? Describe it.

2. What is your favorite holiday? Why?

Directions: *Ask your key pal two more questions about holidays. Write your questions and your key pal's responses in the spaces.*

1.

2.

Group Discussion

Share your key pal's responses with your group.

Holiday Web Site Search

Directions: Search the Web to find sites with information about your favorite holiday. Write down each site's name, URL, features, good points, and bad points. Check a rating for each site.

1. Name of site

URL: http://

Features

Good points

Bad points

Rating ☐ Poor ☐ Fair ☐ Good ☐ Excellent

2. Name of site

URL: http://

Features

Good points

Bad points

Rating ☐ Poor ☐ Fair ☐ Good ☐ Excellent

3. Name of site

URL: http://

Features

Good points

Bad points

Rating ☐ Poor ☐ Fair ☐ Good ☐ Excellent

Writing Activity

Use the information you wrote down to write a review about one of the Web sites. First, describe the site. Then evaluate the site's good points and bad points. Finally, tell your readers whether they should visit the site.

Activity 3

Holiday Hunt

Directions: *What holidays are celebrated around the globe this month? Search the Web to find information about these holidays. Write the information in the spaces.*

1. Holiday

    Date(s)

    Country

2. Holiday

    Date(s)

    Country

3. Holiday

    Date(s)

    Country

4. Holiday

    Date(s)

    Country

5. Holiday

    Date(s)

    Country

6. Holiday

    Date(s)

    Country

7. Holiday

    Date(s)

    Country

8. Holiday

    Date(s)

    Country

Group Discussion

Share your information with your group. Are any of these holidays celebrated in your country? If so, which ones? What other holidays are celebrated in your country this month?

Find That Holiday

Directions: *Search the Web to find information about each of the following holidays. Write the information in the spaces.*

1. Advent   Date(s)   The four weeks before Christmas

Description   A time of preparation for Christmas. Many churches and families have Advent wreaths with candles, and each week a new candle is lit. Some people sing songs or pray.

2. Boxing Day   Date(s)

Description

3. Cinco de Mayo   Date(s)

Description

4. Deepavali   Date(s)

Description

5. Golden Week   Date(s)

Description

6. Lantern Festival   Date(s)

Description

7. Mardi Gras   Date(s)

Description

8. Purim   Date(s)

Description

9. Ramadan   Date(s)

Description

10. Another holiday

Date(s)

Description

11. Another holiday

Date(s)

Description

12. Another holiday

Date(s)

Description

Group Discussion

Share your information with your group. Which of the above holidays interests you the most? Why?

FOLLOW UP

New Vocabulary

Write five new words you learned and their definitions.

1.

2.

3.

4.

5.

Bulletin Board

Post your thoughts about holidays on the Bulletin Board.

Chapter 18 URL Puzzle Clue

What African-American holiday takes place in December? Write the answer in the spaces. Then write the circled letter in the URL Puzzle on page 141.

☐ ☐ ☐ Ⓞ ☐ ☐ ☐

19

Literature

"Literature is my Utopia."

— *Helen Keller*

Activity 1

Key Pal Interchange

***Directions:** Ask your key pal the following questions. Then write the responses in the spaces.*

1. Who is the most famous author in your country? What kinds of books does (or did) this author write?

2. Who is your favorite author? Why?

3. What kinds of books do you enjoy reading? Why?

***Directions:** Ask your key pal two more questions about literature. Write your questions and your key pal's responses in the spaces.*

1.

2.

Group Discussion

Share your key pal's responses with your group.

Author Search

Directions: Search the Web to find information about three living authors, each from a different country. Write the information in the spaces.

1. Name

Nicknames

Birthplace   Date of birth

Family

Education

Other occupations

Novels

Other information

2. Name

Nicknames

Birthplace   Date of birth

Family

Education

Other occupations

Novels

Other information

3. Name

Nicknames

Birthplace   Date of birth

Family

Education

Other occupations

Novels

Other information

Writing Activity

Use the above information to write a paragraph or essay about one of the authors.

Activity 3

The Ten Best English Novels

Directions: *Find the Modern Library Board's ten best English novels of the 20th century. Write the information in the spaces.*

	Title	Author
1.		
2.		
3.		
4.		
5.		
6.		
7.		
8.		
9.		
10.		

Writing Activity

What is the best novel you have ever read? Write a summary of it.

Activity 4

Web-Published Stories

Directions: *Search the Web to find an example of a Web-published story. Read the story. Then write the following information in the spaces.*

Title	
Author	
URL: http://	
Summary	

Group Discussion

Tell your group about the story you read. What is the story about? Did you enjoy reading it? Why or why not? Do you prefer to read Web-published stories or paperback stories? Explain.

FOLLOW UP

New Vocabulary

Write five new words you learned and their definitions.

1.

2.

3.

4.

5.

Bulletin Board

Post your thoughts about literature on the Bulletin Board.

Chapter 19 URL Puzzle Clue

Who wrote *A Catcher in the Rye*? Write the answer in the spaces. Then write the circled letter in the URL Puzzle on page 141.

☐. ☐. ☐Ⓞ☐ ☐ ☐ ☐ ☐ ☐

20 Money

"I have enough money to last me the rest of my life, unless I buy something."

— *Ernest Haskins*

Activity 1

Key Pal Interchange

Directions: *Ask your key pal how much each of the following items costs in his or her country. Then write the responses in the spaces.*

Item	Price	Item	Price
1. Can of soda		**5.** Liter of gasoline	
2. Cup of coffee		**6.** Pair of jeans	
3. City bus ride		**7.** Newspaper	
4. Movie ticket		**8.** Compact disc	

Directions: *Ask your key pal two more questions about prices in his or her country. Write your questions and your key pal's responses in the spaces.*

1.

2.

Group Discussion

Share your key pal's responses with your group.

Foreign Currencies

Directions: *Search the Web to find which countries use the following forms of currency. (**Note:** Some forms of currency are used in more than one country.) Write the information in the spaces.*

Currency	Country	Currency	Country
1. Baht	Thailand	**16.** New peso	
2. Bolivar		**17.** Peseta	
3. Dinar		**18.** Pound	
4. Drachma		**19.** Rand	
5. Escudo		**20.** Real	
6. Forint		**21.** Ringgit	
7. Franc		**22.** Riyal	
8. Guilder		**23.** Ruble	
9. Koruna		**24.** Rupee	
10. Kroner		**25.** Rupiah	
11. Kwacha		**26.** Schilling	
12. Leu		**27.** Shekel	
13. Lev		**28.** Won	
14. Lira		**29.** Yen	
15. Markka		**30.** Zloty	

Group Discussion

Have you ever used any of the above forms of currency? If so, which ones?

Shopping Trip

Directions: *Imagine that you have U.S.$1,000 to spend on items for sale on the Internet. Search the Web to create a shopping list. Write the information in the spaces.*

	Item	Price		Item	Price
1.			**5.**		
2.			**6.**		
3.			**7.**		
4.			**8.**		

Writing Activity

Do you prefer to shop on the Internet or in a store? Explain your reasons in a paragraph or essay.

Activity 4

Time Capsule

Directions: Search the Web to find the average prices of the following items in the United States for each year listed below. Write the information in the spaces.

	1900	1925	1950	1975
1. House	$4,000.00			
2. Car	$500.00			
3. Milk	$.30			
4. Gas	$.05			
5. Bread	$.03			
6. Postage stamp	$.02			

Group Discussion

How much do you think each item costs this year? How much do you think each item will cost in the year 2025? 2050? 2075? 3000? Share your ideas with your group.

FOLLOW UP

New Vocabulary

Write five new words you learned and their definitions.

1.

2.

3.

4.

5.

Bulletin Board

Post your thoughts about money on the Bulletin Board.

Chapter 20 URL Puzzle Clue

What single European Union monetary unit was introduced in January 1999? Write the answer in the spaces. Then write the circled letter in the URL Puzzle on page 141.

BEGIN: `http://www.prenhall.com/sperling`

❝Never judge a book by its movie.❞

—*J. W. Eagan*

Activity 1

Key Pal Interchange

Directions: Ask your key pal the following questions. Then write the responses in the spaces.

1. What kinds of movies do you like?

2. What is your favorite movie? Why?

3. Who is your favorite actor? your favorite actress?

Directions: Ask your key pal two more questions about movies, actors, or actresses. Write your questions and your key pal's responses in the spaces.

1.

2.

Group Discussion

Share your key pal's responses with your group.

The Ten Most Profitable Movies

Directions: Search the Web to find the ten most profitable movies at the international box office. Write the information in the spaces.

Name of Movie	Year Produced
1.	
2.	
3.	
4.	
5.	
6.	
7.	
8.	
9.	
10.	

Writing Activity

Write a review of your favorite movie. First, state the movie's name, genre (type, such as comedy or romance), year released, and stars. Then summarize the movie's plot. Finally, give your opinion of the movie.

Upcoming Movies

Directions: Search the Web to find the titles of three movies that will be released soon. Write the information in the spaces.

1. Name of movie			
Genre		Rating	Release date
Stars			
Other information			

2. Name of movie

Genre		Rating		Release date	

Stars

Other information

3. Name of movie

Genre		Rating		Release date	

Stars

Other information

Group Discussion

Share your information with your group. Which of the movies would you like to see? Why? Which would you not like to see? Why not?

Activity 4

Movie Star Search

Directions: *Search the Web to find information about your favorite movie star. Write the information in the spaces.*

Name of movie star	
Movies	
Interesting facts	

Role Play

Imagine that you are a reporter interviewing a famous movie star. Use the above information to write questions that you would like to ask. Then write possible answers. With a partner, practice the interview. Then role play it for your class.

New Vocabulary

Write five new words you learned and their definitions.

1.

2.

3.

4.

5.

Bulletin Board

Post your thoughts about movies on the Bulletin Board.

Chapter 21 URL Puzzle Clue

In the film *A Boy Named Charlie Brown,* what word does Charlie Brown misspell? Write the answer in the spaces. Then write the circled letter in the URL Puzzle on page 141.

▢ ◯ ▢ ▢ ▢ ▢

BEGIN: | http://www.prenhall.com/sperling

> **"Music . . . can name the unnameable and communicate the unknowable."**
>
> —*Leonard Bernstein*

Activity 1

Key Pal Interchange

Directions: *Ask your key pal the following questions. Then write the responses in the spaces.*

1. What kinds of music do you like? Why?

2. Who is your favorite male singer? your favorite female singer? What are their most popular songs?

3. Who are the most popular musicians in your country?

Directions: *Ask your key pal two more questions about music. Write the questions and the responses in the spaces.*

1.

2.

Group Discussion

Share your key pal's responses with your group.

World Music Search

Directions: Search the Web for information about the following types of music. Write the information in the spaces.

1. Dixieland

Definition | traditional, classic jazz performed by small bands; became popular in '20's

Artists | The Alberts, The Alley Cats, Beachcombers, Dr. Jazz, Jazz Rascals

Other information | The music is marked by two-four rhythm, often accompanied by various stomps and marches. Dixieland bands also preserve 1890's cakewalk music.

2. Flamenco

Definition

Artists

Other information

3. Hip-hop

Definition

Artists

Other information

4. Ska

Definition

Artists

Other information

5. Tejano

Definition

Artists

Other information

6. Zydeco

Definition

Artists

Other information

7. Another type		
Definition		
Artists		
Other information		
8. Another type		
Definition		
Artists		
Other information		

Group Discussion

Share your information with your group. Have you ever listened to any of these types of music? If so, which ones? Which did you like? Why?

Activity 3

Billboard Top 10

Directions: *Search the Web to find the Billboard Top 10 albums. Write the information in the spaces.*

	Artist	Album
1.		
2.		
3.		
4.		
5.		
6.		
7.		
8.		
9.		
10.		

Group Discussion

Do you have any of these albums? If so, which ones? Do you buy many albums? Why or why not? What is your favorite album? Why?

Top Pop Oldies

Directions: Search the Web to find the top pop songs for each of the following years. Write the names of the songs and the artists in the spaces.

	Song	Artist
1960	Theme from A Summer Place	Percy Faith
1961		
1962		
1963		
1964		
1965		
1966		
1967		
1968		
1969		
1970		
1971		
1972		
1973		
1974		
1975		
1976		
1977		
1978		
1979		

Writing Activity

Search the Web for information about a popular singer or songwriter from the '60s or '70s. Write a paragraph or essay about the artist's musical career. Include as many interesting details as possible.

New Vocabulary

Write five new words you learned and their definitions.

1.
2.
3.
4.
5.

Bulletin Board

Post your thoughts about music on the Bulletin Board.

Chapter 22 URL Puzzle Clue

What performer made the song "Blue Suede Shoes" famous? Write the answer in the spaces. Then write the circled letter in the URL Puzzle on page 141.

23

News

BEGIN: http://www.prenhall.com/sperling

> **66** **You should always believe what you read in the newspapers, for that makes them more interesting."**
>
> —*Rose Macauley*

Activity 1

Key Pal Interchange

Directions: Ask your key pal the following questions. Then write the responses in the spaces.

1. Do you read any newspapers or magazines? If so, which ones?

2. Do you prefer the TV news or the radio news? Why?

3. What is today's top news story in your country?

Directions: Ask your key pal two more questions about the news. Write your questions and your key pal's responses in the spaces.

1.

2.

Group Discussion

Share your key pal's responses with your group.

On-line Newspapers

Directions: *Search the Web to find an on-line newspaper. Find the following information and write it in the spaces.*

Name of newspaper	
URL: http://	
Date	
Sections	

Group Discussion

Share your information with your group. Did you enjoy exploring the newspaper? Why or why not? Do you prefer to read on-line newspapers or paper newspapers? Explain.

Activity 3

Headline Search

Directions: *Search the Web to find headlines from five English newspapers from different countries. Write the information in the spaces.*

1. Name of newspaper	
Country	
URL: http://	
Headline	

2. Name of newspaper	
Country	
URL: http://	
Headline	

3. Name of newspaper	
Country	
URL: http://	
Headline	

4. Name of newspaper	
Country	
URL: http://	
Headline	
5. Name of newspaper	
Country	
URL: http://	
Headline	

Group Discussion

Share your information with your group. Use the information in each headline to guess what each article is about. Which headline interests you the most? Why?

Activity 4

News Articles

Directions: *Search the Web to find a news article for each of the following categories. Write the headline for each article in the spaces.*

Category	Headline
1. World news	
2. Business news	
3. Sports news	
4. Entertainment news	
5. Travel news	
6. Health news	

Writing Activity

Choose an article that interests you. Read it. Then write a summary of the article. Be sure to include the main ideas and express them in your own words.

Tabloid Tales

Directions: *A tabloid is "a small newspaper with many pictures and sensational material or rumors." Search the Web to find headlines from five on-line tabloids. Write the name of each tabloid, its URL, and the headline in the spaces.*

1. Tabloid

URL: http://

Headline

2. Tabloid

URL: http://

Headline

3. Tabloid

URL: http://

Headline

4. Tabloid

URL: http://

Headline

5. Tabloid

URL: http://

Headline

 Group Discussion

Share your information with your group. What do you think the stories are about? Which stories do you think are believable? Why? Which do you think are unbelievable? Why?

FOLLOW UP

 New Vocabulary

Write five new words you learned and their definitions.

1.

2.

3.

4.

5.

Bulletin Board

Post your thoughts about the news on the Bulletin Board.

Chapter 23 URL Puzzle Clue

What publicly owned news and information company was established in London in 1851? Write the answer in the spaces. Then write the circled letter in the URL Puzzle on page 141.

BEGIN: http://www.prenhall.com/sperling

"The only normal people are the ones you don't know very well."

—Joe Ancis

Activity 1

Key Pal Interchange

Directions: Ask your key pal the following questions. Then write the responses in the spaces.

1. Who is the most famous person in your country? Why is this person famous?

2. Would you like to be famous? Why or why not?

Directions: Ask your key pal two more questions about people. Write your questions and your key pal's responses in the spaces.

1.

2.

Group Discussion

Share your key pal's responses with your group.

Quotations from Famous People

Directions: *Search the Web for quotations from five famous people. Write the information in the spaces.*

1. Name of person

Quotation

2. Name of person

Quotation

3. Name of person

Quotation

4. Name of person

Quotation

5. Name of person

Quotation

Group Discussion

Share your quotations with your group. What do you think they mean? Do you agree with the ideas expressed? Explain.

Famous People's Birthdays

Directions: *Search the Web to find five famous people who were born on your birthday. Write the following information in the spaces.*

Name of Person	Occupation	Date of Birth
1.		
2.		
3.		
4.		
5.		

Group Discussion

Share your information with your group. Do you think you have much in common with any of these people? Explain.

Activity 4

Most Admired People

Directions: Search the Web to find information about three people that you admire. Write the information in the spaces.

1. Name of person

Occupation

Date of birth   Place of birth

Information about person

2. Name of person

Occupation

Date of birth   Place of birth

Information about person

3. Name of person

Occupation

Date of birth   Place of birth

Information about person

Writing Activity

What person do you admire the most? Why? Explain your reasons in a paragraph or essay.

New Vocabulary

Write five new words you learned and their definitions.

1.

2.

3.

4.

5.

Bulletin Board

Post your thoughts about people on the Bulletin Board.

Chapter 24 URL Puzzle Clue

In what country was Keanu Reeves born? Write the answer in the spaces. Then write the circled letter in the URL Puzzle on page 141.

25 Science

> **❝ The most beautiful thing we can experience is the mysterious. It is the source of all true art and science. ❞**
>
> *—Albert Einstein*

Activity 1

Key Pal Interchange

Directions: *Ask your key pal the following questions. Then write the responses in the spaces.*

1. In your opinion, what is the most important scientific discovery of the twentieth century? Why?

2. Are there any famous scientists from your country? If so, who are they? Why are they famous?

Directions: *Ask your key pal two more questions about science or scientists. Write your questions and your key pal's responses in the spaces.*

1.

2.

Group Discussion

Share your key pal's responses with your group.

Great Scientists

Directions: *Search the Web to find information about five scientists. Write the information in the spaces.*

1. Benjamin Franklin

Date of birth	Jan. 17, 1706	Country	USA

Information about scientist	He was a famous scientist, inventor, statesman, printer, philosopher, musician, and economist.
Discoveries/ Inventions	bifocals, lightning rod, watertight bulkhead, urinary catheter, iron furnace stove, and odometer

2. Marie Curie

Date of birth		Country	

Information about scientist	
Discoveries/ Inventions	

3. Sir Isaac Newton

Date of birth		Country	

Information about scientist	
Discoveries/ Inventions	

4. Thomas Edison

Date of birth		Country	

Information about scientist	
Discoveries/ Inventions	

5. Another scientist

Date of birth		Country	

Information about scientist	
Discoveries/ Inventions	

Role Play

Imagine that you are a reporter interviewing a famous scientist. Use the above information to write questions that you would like to ask. Then write possible answers. With a partner, practice the interview. Then role play it for your class.

Activity 3

Scientific Fields

Directions: Search the Web to find definitions of the following scientific fields. Write the information in the spaces.

1. Archaeology — The scientific study of the material remains of human cultures to derive knowledge about prehistoric and historic times.

2. Astronomy

3. Biology

4. Chemistry

5. Ecology

6. Engineering

7. Geology

8. Mathematics

9. Physics

10. Zoology

Writing Activity

Which scientific field interests you the most? Why? Explain your reasons in a paragraph or essay.

Discoveries and Inventions

Directions: *Search the Web to find the following information about each discovery or invention. Write the information in the spaces.*

Discovery/ Invention	Scientist/Inventor	Country	Year
1. Aspirin	Dr. Felix Hoffman	Germany	1899
2. Bacteria			
3. Chewing gum			
4. DNA			
5. Match			
6. Microscope			
7. Nuclear fission			
8. Ozone			
9. Pen			
10. Solar energy			

Group Discussion

Which invention do you think is the most useful? Why? Rank the discoveries and inventions from the most useful (1) to the least useful (10).

FOLLOW UP

New Vocabulary

Write five new words you learned and their definitions.

1.	
2.	
3.	
4.	
5.	

Bulletin Board

Post your thoughts about people on the Bulletin Board.

Chapter 25 URL Puzzle Clue

Who invented the first stored program concept computer in 1947? Write the answer in the spaces. Then write the circled letter in the URL Puzzle on page 141.

☐ ☐ ☐ ☐   ☐ ☐ ◯   ☐ ☐ ☐ ☐ ☐ ☐ ☐

BEGIN: http://www.prenhall.com/sperling

❝I always turn to the sports page first, which records people's accomplishments. The front page has nothing but man's failures.❞

—*Chief Justice Earl Warren*

Activity 1

Key Pal Interchange

Directions: *Ask your key pal the following questions. Then write the responses in the spaces.*

1. What sports do you like to watch? Why?

2. What sports do you like to play? Why?

Directions: *Ask your key pal two more questions about sports. Write your questions and your responses in the spaces.*

1.

2.

Group Discussion

Share your key pal's responses with your group.

Sports Search

Directions: *Search the Web for three sites on your favorite sport. Write the following information in the spaces.*

1. Name of Web site

URL: http://

Information about sport

2. Name of Web site

URL: http://

Information about sport

3. Name of Web site

URL: http://

Information about sport

 ### Group Discussion

Share your information. What did you already know about the sport? What did you learn?

Types of Sports

Directions: *Search the Web to find definitions of the following sports. Write the information in the spaces.*

Sport	Definition
1. Biathlon	Event with two sports, usually cross-country skiing and target shooting
2. Bobsledding	
3. Cricket	
4. Fencing	
5. Jai alai	
6. Lacrosse	

Sport	Definition
7. Martial arts	
8. Mountain climbing	
9. Polo	
10. Racquetball	

Writing Activity

Which sport interests you the most? Why? Explain your reasons in a paragraph or essay.

Activity 4

Olympic Games Sites

Directions: *Search the Web to find the Olympic Games sites for the following years. Write the information in the spaces.*

Year	Summer Games Site	Winter Games Site
1960	Rome, Italy	Squaw Valley, California, USA
1964		
1968		
1972		
1976		
1980		
1984		
1988		
1992		
1994		
1996		

Group Discussion

What are the advantages to hosting the Olympics? What are the disadvantages? Discuss your ideas.

New Vocabulary

Write five new words you learned and their definitions.

1.

2.

3.

4.

5.

Bulletin Board

Post your thoughts about sports on the Bulletin Board.

Chapter 26 URL Puzzle Clue

What country hosted the first World Cup in 1930? Write the answer in the spaces. Then write the circled letter in the URL Puzzle on page 141.

☐ ☐ ☐ ☐ ☐ ☐ ◯

BEGIN: http://www.prenhall.com/sperling

> **"Thanks to the Interstate Highway System, it is now possible to travel from coast to coast without seeing anything."**
>
> —*Charles Kuralt*

Activity 1

Key Pal Interchange

Directions: *Ask your key pal the following questions. Then write the responses in the spaces.*

1. How do you travel to work or school?

2. What kinds of transportation does your city or town have?

3. Do you own a car? If so, what kind is it? If not, would you like to own a car? Why or why not?

Directions: *Ask your key pal two more questions about amusement parks. Write the questions and the responses in the spaces.*

1.

2.

Group Discussion

Share your key pal's responses with your group.

Types of Transportation

Directions: Search the Web to find definitions of the following types of transportation. Write the information in the spaces.

Transportation	Definition
1. Ferry	A boat for people or vehicles that operates on a regular schedule.
2. Helicopter	
3. Hot air balloon	
4. Kayak	
5. Limousine	
6. Monorail	
7. Steamboat	
8. Streetcar	
9. Submarine	
10. Zeppelin	

Group Discussion

Which of these types of transportation have you used? Describe your experience. Which would you like to try? Why?

Finding a Car

Directions: Search the Web to find a model of each of the following types of cars. Write the following information in the spaces.

1. Compact pickup		**2. Convertible**	
Make	Chevrolet	Make	
Model	1999 S-10	Model	
Base price	$12,802	Base price	
Other information		Other information	
2.2-liter engine, five-speed manual transmission, dual side airbags, anti-lock brakes, power steering			

3. Family sedan

Make _____

Model _____

Base price _____

Other information

_____

4. Minivan

Make _____

Model _____

Base price _____

Other information

_____

5. Sports car

Make _____

Model _____

Base price _____

Other information

_____

6. Station wagon

Make _____

Model _____

Base price _____

Other information

_____

 ## Writing Activity

What type of car do you like the best? Why? Explain your reasons in a paragraph or essay.

Activity 4

Transportation Museums

Directions: *Search the Web to find an on-line transportation museum. Write down the name of the museum, the location, and the URL. Then choose three exhibits that interest you. Write the names and descriptions of the exhibits in the spaces.*

Name of Museum _____

Location _____

URL: http:// _____

1. Name of exhibit _____

Description

_____

2. Name of exhibit

Description

3. Name of exhibit

Description

Group Discussion

Share your information with your group. Why did you choose the museum? Why do the exhibits interest you?

FOLLOW UP

New Vocabulary

Write five new words you learned and their definitions.

1.

2.

3.

4.

5.

Bulletin Board

Post your thoughts about transportation on the Bulletin Board.

Chapter 27 URL Puzzle Clue

What is the name for the magnetized plastic subway card used in the New York subway system? Write the answer in the spaces. Then write the circled letter in the URL Puzzle on page 141.

☐ ☐ ☐ ☐ ☐ Ⓞ ☐ ☐ ☐

66 **Though we travel the world over to find the beautiful, we must carry it with us or we find it not.**"

—*Ralph Waldo Emerson*

Activity 1

Key Pal Interchange

Directions: *Ask your key pal the following questions. Then write the responses in the spaces.*

1. Where did you go on your last vacation? What did you do there?

2. Describe your ideal vacation.

Directions: *Ask your key pal two more questions about travel. Write your questions and your key pal's responses in the spaces.*

1.

2.

Group Discussion

Share your key pal's responses with your group.

Unique Vacations

Directions: Search the Web to find three examples of unique vacations. Write the following information in the spaces.

1. Type of vacation

URL: http://

Location

Features of vacation

2. Type of vacation

URL: http://

Location

Features of vacation

3. Type of vacation

URL: http://

Location

Features of vacation

Writing Activity

Describe your most memorable vacation in a paragraph or essay.

Activity 3

Hotel Search

Directions: Choose a city or town that you would like to visit. Search the Web to find information about three hotels in that city or town. Write the information in the spaces.

City/Town   Country

1. Name of hotel

URL: http://

Address

Telephone number

Rates

Facilities

Other information

2. Name of hotel

URL: http://

Address

Telephone number

Rates

Facilities

Other information

3. Name of hotel

URL: http://

Address

Telephone number

Rates

Facilities

Other information

 Group Discussion

Share your information with your group. Which of the three hotels is the most expensive? the least expensive? Which hotel do you prefer? Why?

Around the World Trip

Directions: *Imagine that you have a year to travel around the world. Search the Web to find flights for a trip around the world that begins and ends in your city. Write the information in the spaces.*

1. Departing from

Your city		Date		Time
	on		at	

Arriving in

Second city		Date		Time
	on		at	

Airline	Class	Price

2. Departing from

Second city		Date		Time
	on		at	

Arriving in

Third city		Date		Time
	on		at	

Airline	Class	Price

3. Departing from

Third city		Date		Time
	on		at	

Arriving in

Fourth city		Date		Time
	on		at	

Airline	Class	Price

4. Departing from

Fourth city		Date		Time
	on		at	

Arriving in

Fifth city		Date		Time
	on		at	

Airline	Class	Price

5. Departing from

Fifth city		Date		Time
	on		at	

Arriving in

Your city		Date		Time
	on		at	

Airline	Class	Price

Group Discussion

Compare your travel plans. What criteria were important to you in your choice of flights? What cities did you decide to visit? Why? How long did you decide to stay in each place? Why?

FOLLOW UP

New Vocabulary

Write five new words you learned and their definitions.

1.

2.

3.

4.

5.

Bulletin Board

Post your thoughts about travel on the Bulletin Board.

Chapter 28 URL Puzzle Clue

In what state did the first hostel of the American Youth Hostels (AYH) open? Write the answer in the spaces. Then write the circled letter in the URL Puzzle on page 141.

□ □ □ □ □ □ □ □ Ⓞ □ □ □ □

29

Wea

weather

Weather

> **"Weather is a great bluffer. I guess the same is true of our human society -- things can look dark, then a break shows in the clouds, and all is changed."**
>
> —*E. B. White*

Activity 1

Key Pal Interchange

Directions: Ask your key pal the following questions. Then write the responses in the spaces.

1. How is the weather today in your city?

2. What kind of weather do you like? Why?

3. What kind of weather do you dislike? Why?

Directions: Ask your key pal two more questions about weather. Write the questions and the responses in the spaces.

1.

2.

Group Discussion

Share your key pal's responses with your group.

Weather Report

Directions: *Search the Web to find this week's weather forecast for your city. Write the information in the spaces.*

Name of city _____

Date	Weather	High Temperature	Low Temperature
Today			
Tomorrow			
Day of week ____			
Day of week ____			
Day of week ____			

Group Discussion

Do you think the weather forecast will affect any of your plans for this week? Explain.

Weather Around the Globe

Directions: *Search the Web to find tomorrow's weather forecast for each of the following cities. Write the information in the spaces.*

City	Weather	High Temperature	Low Temperature
1. Bombay			
2. Buenos Aires			
3. Honolulu			
4. Madrid			
5. Mexico City			
6. Montreal			
7. Nairobi			
8. Oslo			
9. Sydney			
10. Vancouver			

Group Discussion

Which city is the hottest? the coldest? Which city's weather do you like the most? Why? Which city's weather do you like the least? Why?

Activity 4

World's Highest and Lowest Temperatures

Directions: *Search the Web to find the highest and lowest recorded temperatures for each of the following continents. Write the information in the spaces.*

Continent		Specific Location	Date
1. Africa			
Highest Temperature			
Lowest Temperature			
2. Antarctica			
Highest Temperature			
Lowest Temperature			
3. Asia			
Highest Temperature			
Lowest Temperature			
4. Australia			
Highest Temperature			
Lowest Temperature			
5. Europe			
Highest Temperature			
Lowest Temperature			
6. North America			
Highest Temperature			
Lowest Temperature			
7. South America			
Highest Temperature			
Lowest Temperature			

Group Discussion

In your opinion, what is the highest temperature in which people can survive? the lowest temperature? What is the highest temperature you have ever experienced? the lowest temperature?

Extreme Weather Conditions

Directions: Search the Web to find examples of each of the following extreme weather conditions. Write the following information in the spaces.

1. Avalanche

Date(s)	November 25, 1997
Location	North Gallatin Range, Bozeman, MT
Details	A skier caused the avalanche, but was not caught.

2. Blizzard

Date(s)	
Location	
Details	

3. Cyclone

Date(s)	
Location	
Details	

4. Drought

Date(s)	
Location	
Details	

5. Flood

Date(s)	
Location	
Details	

6. Hurricane

Date(s)	
Location	
Details	

7. Lightning

Date(s)

Location

Details

8. Tornado

Date(s)

Location

Details

9. Tsunami

Date(s)

Location

Details

10. Typhoon

Date(s)

Location

Details

Writing Activity

What is the most extreme or unusual weather you have ever experienced?
Describe the event in a paragraph or essay.

FOLLOW UP

New Vocabulary

Write five new words you learned and their definitions.

1.

2.

3.

4.

5.

Bulletin Board

Post your thoughts about weather on the Bulletin Board.

Chapter 29 URL Puzzle Clue

According to American legend, what animal forecasts six more weeks of winter if it sees its shadow on February 2? Write the answer in the spaces. Then write the circled letter in the URL Puzzle on page 141.

☐ ◯ ☐ ☐ ☐ ☐ ☐ ☐ ☐

30 Work

> **"It is your work in life that is the ultimate seduction."**
>
> —*Pablo Picasso*

Activity 1

Key Pal Interchange

Directions: *Ask your key pal the following questions. Then write the responses in the spaces.*

1. Do you have a job? If so, what is it?

2. Describe your ideal job.

3. What are some popular occupations in your country?

Directions: *Ask your key pal two more questions about work. Write your questions and your key pal's responses in the spaces.*

1.

2.

Group Discussion

Share your key pal's responses with your group.

Types of Interviews

Directions: Search the Web to find definitions of the following types of interviews. Write the information in the spaces.

1. Group interview

It usually consists of three or more people, all asking questions. It is also referred to as a panel interview.

2. In-person screening interview

3. Luncheon interview

4. Peer group interview

5. Selection interview

6. Stress interview

7. Telephone screening interview

8. Video conference interview

9. Work sample interview

 Group Discussion

Which type of interview do you prefer? Why? Which type of interview is the most common in your country? Have you ever had a job interview? If so, describe it.

Job Interview Questions

Directions: Search the Web to find ten common interview questions. Write them in the spaces.

1.	Why do you want to work here?
2.	
3.	
4.	
5.	
6.	
7.	
8.	
9.	
10.	

Role Play

Imagine that you have an interview for your ideal job. Prepare answers for the above questions and write questions to ask the employer. With a partner, practice the interview. Then role play it for your class.

Summer Jobs

Directions: Choose three countries where you would like to work. Search the Web to find a summer job in each country. Write the information in the spaces.

1. Country	
Job title	
Location	
Job description	
Qualifications	

2. Country

Job title

Location

Job
description

Qualifications

3. Country

Job title

Location

Job
description

Qualifications

Writing Activity

Write a paragraph or essay about your ideal job.

FOLLOW UP

New Vocabulary

Write five new words you learned and their definitions.

1.

2.

3.

4.

5.

Bulletin Board

Post your thoughts about work on the Bulletin Board.

Chapter 30 URL Puzzle Clue

What is the word for "a system that allows employees to choose their own times for starting and finishing work"? Write the answer in the spaces. Then write the circled letter in the URL Puzzle on page 141.

☐ ☐ ◯ ☐ ☐ ☐ ☐ ☐

URL puzzle

URL Puzzle

BEGIN: http://www.prenhall.com/sperling

Directions: *Use the URL Puzzle Clues at the end of each chapter to solve this puzzle.*

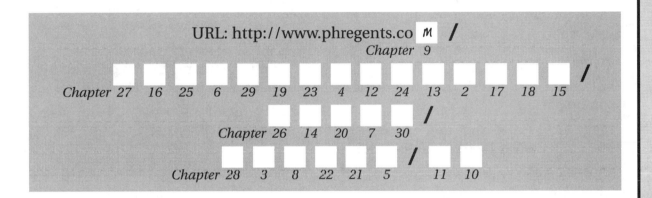

When you have finished, go the URL Puzzle Page. Type in your answer and then submit it. If it is correct, you will gain access to **Dave Sperling's Secret Web Site!**

Glossary of Internet Terms

attachment File, graphics, or software that can be included with an e-mail message.

Bcc Blind carbon copy. A copy of an e-mail message sent secretly to a person other than the primary recipient.

body The message area of an e-mail message.

bookmark A marker that enables the user to return to a Web page at a later date. Also called **favorite**.

bounced message E-mail that is returned when it cannot reach its destination in cyberspace.

browser See **Web browser**.

bulletin board A Web page where messages can be posted.

Cc Carbon Copy. An e-mail message sent to a person other than the primary recipient.

chat A way of communicating in real time with other Internet users.

commercial service One of the large online services, such as America Online, CompuServe, and Prodigy.

cyberspace The "world" of computer networks, in particular the Internet.

dial-up connection A connection to the Internet via a modem.

domain name The part of an Internet address to the right of the @ sign, such as `aol.com` or `hotmail.com`.

dot The word used instead of a period when saying an Internet address. For example, "My home page is eslcafe dot com."

download To transfer a file from one computer to another, usually via a modem.

e-mail Electronic mail. Messages sent over the Internet.

emoticon Emotion icon. Text used to show emotion and humor in Internet messages. Also called **Smiley**.

favorite See **bookmark**.

flame To angrily and unreasonably attack another person over the Internet.

GIF Graphical Interchange Format. A convenient way to store pictures on the Internet.

gopher A menu-driven guide to Internet directories, organized by subject.

hit A request to a Web server to send a particular file. When a user visits a Web page, he or she makes one "hit."

home page The main page of the Web site of an individual, group, or organization.

HTML HyperText Markup Language. The language used to create documents on the World Wide Web.

hyperlink Clickable text on a Web page that will take the user to another Web page.

Internet The largest interconnected network of computers in the world.

Internet Service Provider (ISP) A company or organization that offers access to the Internet.

key pal A pen pal who communicates via e-mail.

link See **hyperlink**.

listserv A mailing list program that automatically sends e-mail to a group of subscribers.

mailing list A list of people who subscribe to a discussion forum and receive email on a specific topic.

Microsoft Explorer One of the most popular Web browsers.

modem A device that links one computer to another over standard telephone lines.

Net Abbreviation for "Internet."

netiquette Net etiquette. Good manners on the Internet.

netizen Net citizen. A member of the Internet community.

Netscape Navigator One of the most popular Web browsers.

newsgroup A USENET message area where the user can discuss a specific topic.

off-line Disconnected from the Internet.

on-line Connected to the Internet.

password A secret code needed to enter a computer system.

PPP Point-to-Point Protocol. A way to browse the Web over a phone line.

public domain Material not protected by copyright law, which can be used freely without permission.

real time The Internet term for something live, such as Internet Relay Chat (IRC).

search engine An Internet tool that helps locate information.

server A computer that provides a specific service, such as e-mail, gopher, or the World Wide Web.

shareware Software that can be downloaded for free.

Smiley See **emoticon**.

SMTP Simple Mail Transfer Protocol. The language that a mail server uses to send and receive e-mail on the Internet.

snail mail Mail delivered (slowly) via the post office.

SPAM Sending Particularly Annoying Messages. Sending a single message to multiple mailing lists. SPAM is bad netiquette.

surf To search the Net.

telnet A program that allows the user to access a computer or server from a remote computer.

thread Replies to a particular newsgroup message.

upload To transfer a file from one's local computer to a remote computer.

URL Uniform Resource Locator, pronounced U-R-L. A World Wide Web address. For example, `http://www.eslcafe.com` is the URL of my home page, Dave's ESL Café.

USENET A collection of thousands of newgroups for exchanging messages on different topics.

user name The unique account name given to a user on a system. My user name, for example, is `sperling`.

virus A damaging program that is transferred from one computer to another computer via phone lines or floppy disks. Virus-scanning software can usually prevent this problem.

Web See **World Wide Web**.

Web browser A program that allows people to navigate and view the World Wide Web. Netscape and Microsoft Explorer are the most popular browsers.

Web page A document at a specific URL on the World Wide Web.

Web site A set of connected Web pages of an individual, group, or organization.

World Wide Web A collection of inter-connected documents. Also called the **Web**, the World Wide Web is becoming the most popular area of the Internet.

Yahoo One of the oldest and most popular search directories on the World Wide Web.